Exploring Citizenship

Leadership

Sue Barraclough

Heinemann Library,
Chicago, IL

www.heinemannraintree.com

Visit our website to find out more information about Heinemann-Raintree books.

To order:

☎ Phone 888-454-2279

⌨ Visit www.heinemannraintree.com to browse our catalog and order online.

©2010 Heinemann Library
an imprint of Capstone Global Library, LLC
Chicago, Illinois

Edited by Rebecca Rissman and Catherine Veitch
Designed by Ryan Frieson and Betsy Wernert
Picture research by Elizabeth Alexander and Rebecca Sodergren
Production by Duncan Gilbert
Originated by Heinemann Library
Printed in China by South China Printing Company Ltd

Library of Congress Cataloging-in-Publication Data
Barraclough, Sue.
  Leadership / Sue Barraclough. -- 1st ed.
      p. cm.
  Includes bibliographical references and index.
  ISBN 978-1-4329-3314-2 (hc) -- ISBN 978-1-4329-3322-7 (pb) 1.
Leadership. I. Title.
  HM1261.B38 2009
  303.3'4--dc22
                                    2008055302

Acknowledgments

We would like to thank the following for permission to reproduce photographs: Alamy **pp. 5** (© Jupiterimages/Bananastock), **11** (© Kim Karpeles), **8** (© Picture Partners), **9** (© Janine Wiedel Photolibrary), **13** (© Jeff Greenberg), **29** (© Steve Skjold); © Corbis **p. 10**; Corbis **pp. 4** (© Kevin Dodge), **16** (© Lacy Atkins/San Francisco Chronicle), **21** (© Rolf Bruderer), **22** (© Andersen Ross/Blend Images), **23** (© Jupiterimages/Brand X), **24** (© Tannen Maury/epa), **27** (© William Gottlieb); Getty Images **pp. 7** (Paul Harris/Stone), **12** (Justin Sullivan), **17** (Alistair Berg/Photonica), **18** (Photo & Co/Stone); Photolibrary **pp. 6** (Radius images), **26** (Radius images), **20** (Design Pics Inc.), **25** (Rob Crandall), **14** (SW Productions/Photodisc).

Cover photograph of a family hiking in the woods reproduced with permission of Corbis (© image100).

The publishers would like to thank Yael Biederman for her help in the preparation of this book.

Every effort has been made to contact copyright holders of any material reproduced in this book. Any omissions will be rectified in subsequent printings if notice is given to the publisher.

Contents

Some words are shown in bold, **like this**. You can find out what they mean by looking in the glossary.

What Is Citizenship?

Citizenship is about being a member of a group. A group can be a family, a school, a team, or a country. As a member of a group, you have certain **rights** and **responsibilities**.

It is good to be a member of a group that has fun together.

It is good citizenship to take care of younger children.

Having rights means there are certain ways other people should treat you. Having responsibilities means you should act or behave in a certain way.

What Is a Leader?

A leader is someone you follow. A leader shows the way by going first. A leader is usually someone who knows which way to go.

A good leader can show you what to do.

You can often learn from a leader.

Leadership means being in charge or in control. Being a leader means you have the power to act for a group. A leader sometimes makes some decisions for a group.

Why Do We Need Leaders?

It can be hard for a large group to agree unless one person takes the lead.

Leaders can help people make decisions. When a group of people has to decide on something, a leader can help everybody choose what to do or where to go.

It is sometimes useful to have a leader who makes decisions with a group. A leader can decide to do what is best for most people in a group. This is a **fair** way to make a decision.

It is easier for a big group if one person leads the way.

What Makes a Good Leader?

Anyone can be a leader, but parents or adults are often leaders. They have **experience** that helps them make good choices and decisions.

As a child you **trust** your parents or grandparents to make decisions or choices for your family group.

A teacher is the leader of a class. A teacher is in charge of taking care of a class and has **knowledge** to share.

It is important to listen when a leader is talking to a group.

Honesty and Fairness

A good leader is honest. Honesty is always telling the truth and doing what you say you will. A leader is in charge of a group, so it is important that people can **trust** the person to be honest and **fair**.

Why is it important for leaders to be honest?

Good leaders listen so they know what people need.

Fairness is treating everyone **equally**. A fair leader chooses to do what is best for most people. Good leaders try to make sure that decisions are fair to everyone.

Good Communication

A good leader **communicates** well. This means good leaders speak clearly and listen well. They also make sure everyone understands them.

Good leaders listen to everyone.

Good communication is an important leadership **skill**.

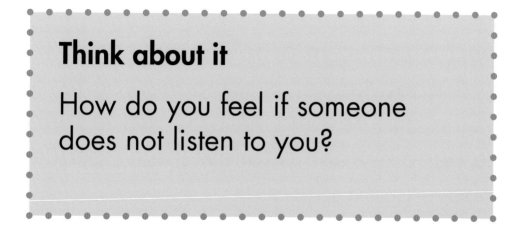

Tips for good communication

- ☑ speak clearly
- ☑ stay calm and do not shout or get angry
- ☑ explain ideas clearly
- ☑ listen carefully
- ☑ ask questions and discuss

Think about it

How do you feel if someone does not listen to you?

Respect

A good leader needs to show and earn respect.

Respect is acting in a polite and caring way. A good leader is someone you respect and who also respects you. Good leaders make people want to follow them because they have good ideas.

A leader such as a sports coach is in charge because he or she has **knowledge** or **experience** to share with players. A leader earns respect by having good ideas and problem-solving **skills**.

A good leader takes the time to explain things clearly.

A Role Model

A **role model** is someone you **admire** and whose behavior you want to copy. A good leader leads by making you want to do well. A good leader makes you feel good about yourself.

People feel better following a leader who believes they can do well.

A good leader sets a good example to follow and shows you what to do. Leaders lead better by working with the group and behaving well.

Tips for helping a group or team do well

- ☑ say "good job!"
- ☑ **communicate** with everyone
- ☑ set a good example
- ☑ be **enthusiastic**
- ☑ show that you value the team

Leading and Following

A good leader does not shout at you or bully you. Bad leaders use **fear** to make people follow them.

A good leader is not a bully.

Think about it

Do you think you would be happier to have a strong, **fair**, and kind leader? Or would you rather have a leader who is cruel and unfair?

Remember that younger children might expect you to be a leader.

Taking Responsibility

You have a responsibility to take part and to know how you want to be treated.

As a member of a group, you may have a **responsibility** to take part in choosing leaders. You also have a **right** to say if you think leaders are doing a good job.

If you are unhappy, you need to say what you would like to change.

A leader cannot know you are unhappy if you do not say so. It is not easy being a leader. It is not always easy to make decisions for other people.

Choosing a Leader

In most countries, leaders are chosen by the people of that country. All the people **vote** to choose the person or people to be in charge of the country in an **election**.

We choose leaders who we think will make good decisions for us.

Choosing a leader is an important **responsibility**.

When you are older, you will get the chance to choose leaders in your local community and for your country, too. In school you should get a chance to take part in a student council or learn leadership **skills** on sports teams.

Speaking Out

What do you think makes a good leader of a group?

As a leader of a group or team, you need to be able to explain your ideas and decisions. You also need to listen to members of the group and answer questions.

Leaders need to speak out against cruelty or unfairness. Being a leader can be difficult because people will not always like your decisions. You have to believe that you are doing the right thing.

If you think someone is being treated unkindly, you should say so.

Is Leadership Important?

It is important to learn good leadership **skills**. You have a **responsibility** to take part in different groups. You should understand your **right** to make your own choices.

A good leader:

- ☑ **respects** and listens to others
- ☑ acts honestly and **fairly**
- ☑ **communicates** well
- ☑ is a good **role model**

Learning to lead is an important part of growing up. It is important to take the lead, even if it makes you feel nervous. Everyone should try being a leader to understand what it means.

Student councils are a chance to learn leadership skills. Everyone has the chance to speak.

Glossary

admire respect and like someone

communicate speak and listen

election time when people vote to choose a leader

enthusiastic interested and excited about something

equal same in importance (to have the same rights)

experience knowledge or skill gained by doing, learning, or feeling

fair way of behaving that treats everyone equally and that everyone is happy with

fear being frightened of someone or something

knowledge understanding and facts

respect way of treating someone or something with kindness and politeness

responsibility something that it is your job to do as a good and useful member of a group

right how you should be treated by others, in a way that is thought to be good or fair by most people

role model someone you admire. A role model is a person whose behavior you try to copy.

skill being able to do something well

trust know someone is honest and fair

vote make a choice, usually by marking a paper or holding up your hand

Find Out More

Books

Loewen, Nancy. *Do I Have To?: Kids Talk About Responsibility*. Mankato, Minn.: Picture Window, 2003.

Mayer, Cassie. *Being a Leader*. Chicago: Heinemann Library, 2008.

Mayer, Cassie. *Being Responsible*. Chicago: Heinemann Library, 2008.

Small, Mary. Being a Good Citizen: A Book About Citizenship Mankato, Minn.: Picture Window, 2006.

Websites

www.hud.gov/kids
This Website shows children what it means to be good citizens.

www.nasc.us
The Website of the National Association of Student Councils offers ideas and activities that could help you with your own student council.

Index